Famil

La famille

lah fam-*ee*

Illustrated by Clare Beaton

Illustré par Clare Beaton

mother
mummy

la mère

lah mair

maman

ma-*moh*

father
daddy

le père

ler pair

papa

pa-p*ah*

parents

les parents

leh pah-*roh*

sister

la sœur

lah sir

brother

le frère

ler frair

uncle

l'oncle

lonkl'

aunt

la tante

lah tah–t

cousins

les cousins

leh coo-*zah*

grandmother
grandma

la grand-mère

lah groh-*mair*

mémé

mem-*eh*

grandfather
grandpa

le grand-père

ler groh-*pair*

pépé

pep-*eh*

grandparents

les grands-parents

leh groh-par-*roh*

A simple guide to pronouncing the French words

- Read this guide as naturally as possible, as if it were British English of a generally South-Eastern variety (so-called RP).
- Put stress on the letters in *italics* e.g. lombool-*onss*.
- Don't roll the r at the end of the word, for example in the French word le (the): ler.

La famille	lah fam-*ee*	**Family**
la mère	lah mair	**mother**
maman	ma-*moh*	**mummy**
le père	ler pair	**father**
papa	pa-*pah*	**daddy**
les parents	leh pah-*roh*	**parents**
la sœur	lah sir	**sister**
le frère	ler frair	**brother**
l'oncle	lonkl'	**uncle**
la tante	lah tah-t	**aunt**
les cousins	leh coo-*zah*	**cousins**
la grand-mère	lah groh-*mair*	**grandmother**
mémé	mem-*eh*	**grandma**
le grand-père	ler groh-pair	**grandfather**
pépé	pep-*eh*	**grandpa**
les grands-parents	leh groh-par-*roh*	**grandparents**

Published by b small publishing
The Book Shed, 36 Leyborne Park, Kew, Richmond, Surrey, TW9 3HA, UK
www.bsmall.co.uk
© b small publishing, 1994 and 2008 (new cover)
4 5 6
All rights reserved.
Printed in China by WKT Company Ltd.
ISBN-13: 978-1-874735-75-5 (UK paperback)
Cataloguing-in-Publication Data:
A catalogue record for this book is available from the British Library

A & M

forever...

First published in hardback in Great Britain by HarperCollins Children's Books in 2005
First published in paperback in 2005
This edition published in 2011

5 7 9 10 8 6 4

ISBN: 978-0-00-718407-1

HarperCollins Children's Books is a division of HarperCollins Publishers Ltd.

Text and illustrations copyright © Mandy Stanley 2005

Visit our website at: www.harpercollins.co.uk

Printed in China By South China Printing Co. Ltd

Lettice

The Bridesmaid

Mandy Stanley

HarperCollins *Children's Books*

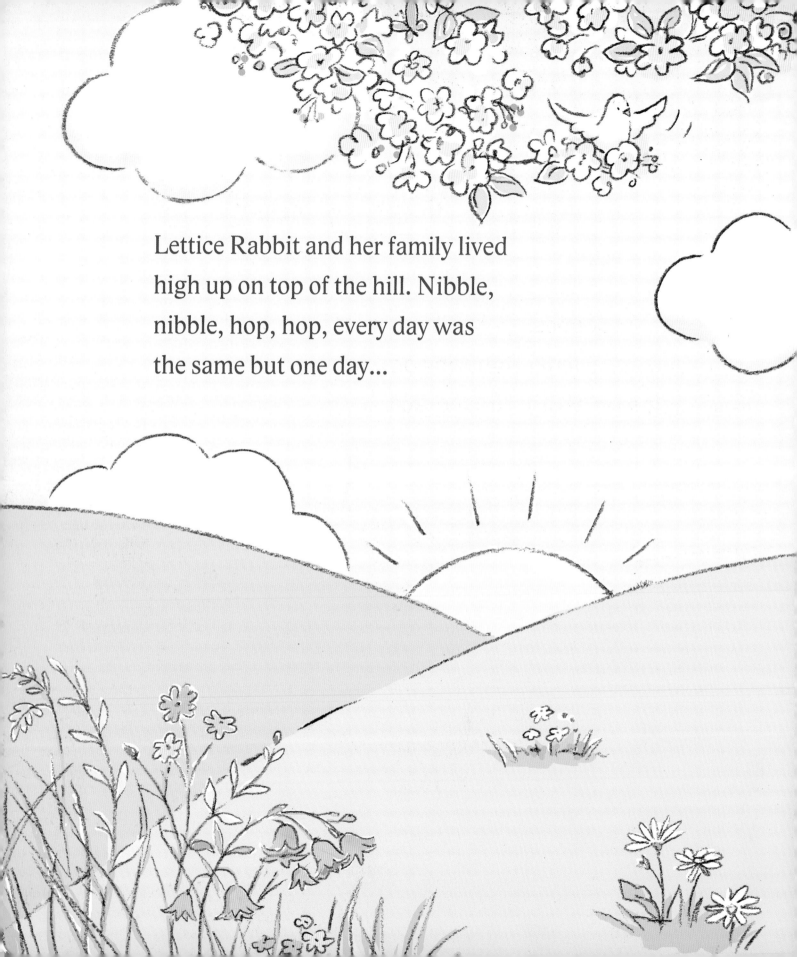

Lettice Rabbit and her family lived
high up on top of the hill. Nibble,
nibble, hop, hop, every day was
the same but one day...

Lettice popped her head out of the burrow
and saw a letter fluttering on a bush.
'It's for ME!' she squeaked.

Paws shaking, Lettice opened the letter.
It said:

Dear Lettice

I am getting married very soon.
Will you be my bridesmaid?
Come and see me today and I'll tell you all about it.

Love
Your dancing teacher
Giselle xxx

Lettice wiggled with excitement.
A bridesmaid! What was that?

She scampered
over the hill to her
dancing teacher's house.

'Come in, Lettice,'
laughed Giselle.
'I've got something
special to
show you!'

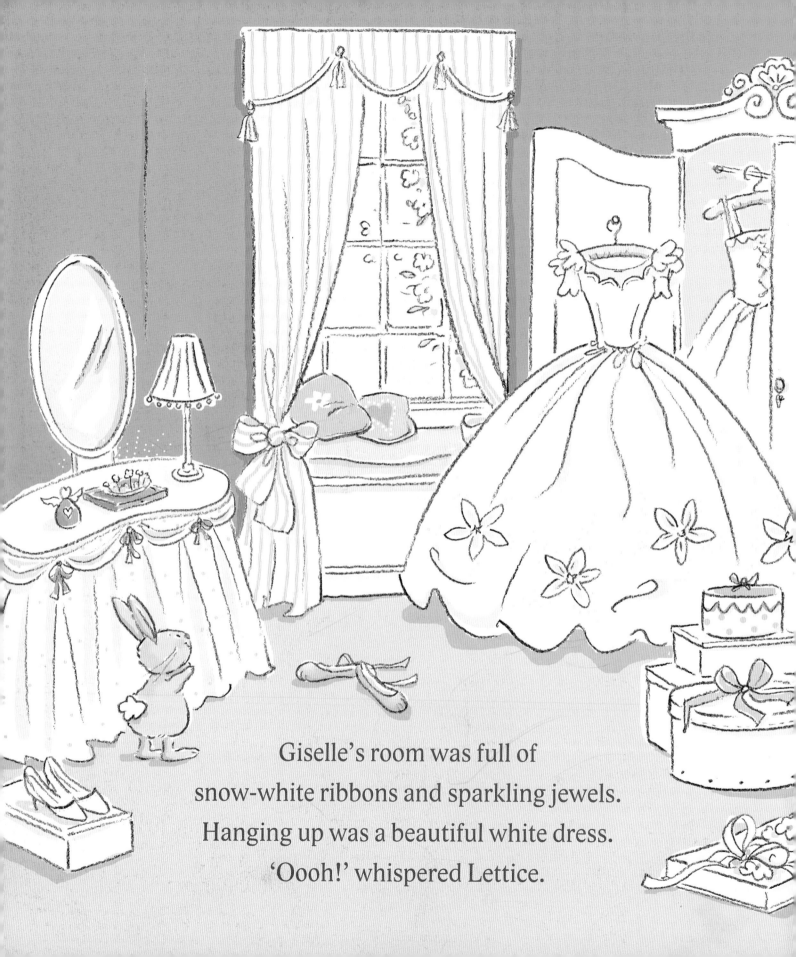

Giselle's room was full of
snow-white ribbons and sparkling jewels.
Hanging up was a beautiful white dress.
'Oooh!' whispered Lettice.

Suddenly, the dress twitched. Lettice stared as two hands appeared.

A boy scrambled out from under the dress.
  'This is Harry. He's going to be my
ring bearer at the wedding,'
said Giselle.

'Harry,' said Giselle, 'on the day, my wedding ring will be placed on this cushion, which I'd like you to carry.'

Then she gave Lettice
a basket and explained,
'You will scatter flowers in
front of me as I arrive
to get married.'

Next, Lettice was measured
for her bridesmaid's dress.
'It'll be made especially
for you,' said Giselle.

Lettice raced home with an invitation
for the whole family. She couldn't
wait to tell everyone all about
the wedding.

On the morning of the
wedding, Lettice got
up very early.

Her mother was
getting the little
ones ready.

Soon it was time to leave.

Lettice hopped across the meadow,
gathering the prettiest flowers
for her basket.

Giselle looked beautiful in her wedding dress.

'Harry,' said Giselle.
'Here is the ring.
Don't lose it!'

'Come with me, Lettice,'
she smiled. 'It's time for
you to put on your
bridesmaid's dress.'

Gently, Lettice unwrapped her clothes. 'Just for me?' she whispered.

First, she wiggled into the petticoat...

then she tied the ribbons on her slippers...

...and placed some flowers on her ears.

Finally, Lettice put on her new dress.

'Now I really am a bridesmaid!' she sighed, swishing the skirt.

At last it was time for the wedding to begin.
Lettice took a deep breath and scattered her
flowers. They flew up in a coloured cloud.
As Giselle walked by, Lettice waited for Harry.

But Harry looked very worried.
'The ring!' he gasped.
'It's GONE!'
Lettice couldn't
believe her ears.

Quickly, they
searched along the
gravel path...

and in amongst
the flowers.
Harry began
to cry.

Just as he pulled out his
handkerchief, Lettice saw
something glinting.

'The ring!' she shrieked.
'It must have slipped into your pocket!
Quickly, we must catch up with Giselle!'

George beamed with happiness as he
saw his bride arrive with Lettice and Harry.

And when Giselle said, 'I do,' everyone sighed.
It was the most beautiful wedding they had ever seen.

Later, Giselle had presents for Lettice and Harry.
'I want to thank you both for helping to make this
the happiest day of my life,' she said.

'And I have a
present for you,'
said Lettice.

She twirled and
whirled...

...and spun around in
her own special dance,
just for Giselle.

The moon was up by the time Lettice and her
family set off home. Lettice was so tired that
her father had to carry her to their burrow.

'It's been a perfect day,' she whispered sleepily.
'The most perfect day of my life.'

Lettice

More dreams come true for
Lettice Rabbit in these
adorable picture books!

Lettice – The Dancing Rabbit
PB: 978-0-00-664777-5

Lettice – A Christmas Wish
PB: 978-0-00-716585-8

Lettice –The Fairy Ball
PB: 978-0-00-720195-2